What others have to say about Captain Frank A. Erickson, USC

"Some heroes don't just happen in a flash or bang. Nor are some heroes' efforts spotted soon enough that they are properly recognized in their lifetime. This is that story. Captain Frank A. Erickson, US Coast Guard, dedicated himself to an idea few liked: a useless helicopter. His career's self-sacrifice ended with a surprising result that eventually saved hundreds of thousands of lives—and lives saved will continue forever where people are endangered by nature's attacks and accidents. This is his story for everyone."

> - Tom Beard, former Coast Guard helicopter rescue pilot
> and author of *Wonderful Flying Machines.*

"Jim Brewster brings to life a little known chapter in aviation as well as Coast Guard history. Few of us in the Baby Boom generation, and fans of the hit TV show *MASH,* realize that it was less than 10 years preceding the Korean War that the first helicopter was put into service in the dramatic lifesaving role portrayed in that show. As a career helicopter pilot in both the U.S. Coast Guard and the Maryland State Police, I've had the honor of personally witnessing CAPT Erickson's dream of vertical lift rescue come true. Coast Guard aviators had been saving lives long before CAPT Erickson's historic flight in 1944, but that momentous event led to a new chapter in both wartime and peacetime Search and Rescue around the world. This is a true story that every young boy and girl, as well as their parents, should enjoy."

> - LCDR Rick Bartlett, USCG, Retired

"A wonderfully well-written story of CAPT Frank Erickson's heroism and innovation which shows why he is a sterling example of the Coast Guard's core value of 'Devotion to Duty.' Erickson's proactive involvement in the field of aviation and perfecting the use of the helicopter as a search and rescue instrument has resulted in the saving of thousands of lives. Easy to read and understand why the Coast Guard revere's the achievements of CAPT Frank Erickson."

> - Vince Patton, MCPOCG, USCG, Retired

HEROES OF THE COAST GUARD

Captain Frank A. Erickson, USCG - Helicopter Pilot No. 1

Written by **James Burd Brewster**

Illustrations by Matthew Melillo

J2B Publishing

Also by James Burd Brewster

Who Wants a Cookie?

Poppa's Pics

"Glad to do it!" Books (ages 3 -7)

Uncle Rocky, Fireman #1 - *Fire!*

Uncle Rocky, Fireman #2 - *Something's Missing*

Uncle Rocky, Fireman #3 - *Sparky's Rescue*

Uncle Rocky, Fireman #4 - *Sparky Protects*

Uncle Rocky, Fireman #5 - *Picnic*

Uncle Rocky, Fireman #6 - *Face Mask*

Uncle Rocky, Fireman #7 - *Safe at Home*

Officer Jack - Book 1 - *Lost Lady*

Officer Jack - Book 2 - *Underwater*

Officer Jack - Book 3 - *Rapid Response*

Officer Jack - Book 4 - *Stolen Puppy*

HEROES OF THE COAST GUARD

Captain Frank A. Erickson, USCG - Helicopter Pilot No. 1

Written by James Burd Brewster   Illustrations by Matthew Melillo

J2B Publishing

Edited by Stephen Rich
Interior Design by Mary Barrows
Cover Design by Jim Taff

USCG Aviation Centennial Logo provided courtesy of the U. S. Coast Guard.
100th Anniversary logo and CGAA graphics courtesy of Coast Guard Aviation Association - www.aoptero.org.

We hope you enjoy this "Heroes of the Coast Guard" book from J2B Publishing. Our goal is to provide "good books for young boys and girls"—books that honor public service and devotion to duty while also encouraging humility when praised for doing one's duty. For more information on the "Heroes of the Coast Guard" or "Glad to do it!" books, please visit www.gladtodoit.net or write to:

J2B Publishing LLC
4251 Columbia Park Road
Pomfret, MD 20675
GladToDoIt@gmail.com
202-557-8097

ISBN: Paperback   978-1-941927-36-6
             Casebound   978-1-941927-37-3

Printed and bound in the United States of America.

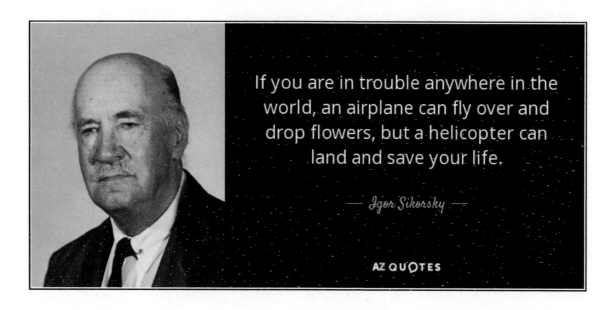

If you are in trouble anywhere in the world, an airplane can fly over and drop flowers, but a helicopter can land and save your life.

— *Igor Sikorsky* —

AZ QUOTES

"… as far as my own part in helicopter development is concerned, it has been the life-saving aspect of the helicopter accomplishments that has given me the greatest personal satisfaction."

- Igor Sikorsky

Contents:

Introduction

Captain Frank A. Erickson's first Life Flight came to my attention while assigned in late 1992 to the 50th Anniversary of World War II Commemoration Committee. My job was to identify important United States Coast Guard World War II actions, events, and participants, and include them in the national remembrance program.

Dr. Robert Browning and Mr. Scott Price of the USCG Historian's Office welcomed me with open arms and open files. My reading soon took me to CAPT Erickson, his development of the helicopter, and the first helicopter "Life Flight" on January 3, 1944. Erickson's Life Flight was not only a unique WWII event, but remains significant today to the hundreds of thousands of people who have been saved by helicopters since then. Impressed by this singular accomplishment, I wrote a fact sheet titled "The Coast Guard and the First Helicopter 'Life Flight'" for the WWII Commemorative Community Program.

More has been written about Erickson since then, particularly Barrett Thomas Beard's *Wonderful Flying Machines: A History of U.S. Coast Guard Helicopters.* On page 179, he quotes Igor Sikorsky, the inventor of the helicopter:

> "Captain Erickson was one of the earliest to foresee the life-saving potential of the helicopter, especially for use in situations where anything but a vertical lift aircraft would be too little or too late. But he was more than a visionary; he was an activist who, after learning to fly a helicopter in 1942, devoted the remainder of his Coast Guard career to promoting, recommending and demonstrating the life-saving capabilities of the helicopter."

I joined and served a full career in the Coast Guard because its fundamental purpose is to save lives in peril on the sea. My love for the organization only deepened when I learned that Erickson, one of our own, first saw the helicopter's potential, developed it into the rescue tool it now is, and persevered until the Coast Guard adopted it.

This book is published on the 72nd Anniversary of Erickson's ground breaking flight to honor Erickson and remind today's helicopter pilots that they owe their profession and wonderful reputation to CAPT Frank A. Erickson, USCG.

It is my belief that Jan 3, 1944 should be remembered each year as the inauguration of the Life Flight.

Chapter 1 - *First Life Flight*

Author Note: Most of the historical conversations in this book are my creation, however the points they make and the information they convey are accurate to the events depicted.

BOOM! The concussive force of a distant explosion hammered the walls of the Coast Guard helicopter hangar. The big doors shuddered and the windows rattled.

"What was that?" exclaimed Commander (CDR) Frank Arthur Erickson, pilot of the dark blue Sikorsky HNS-1 helicopter in front of him. Painted on the side in big white font was the number 445.

"That was a big explosion," said Lieutenant (LT) Walter Bolton, his co-pilot.

They both looked at their watches and then glanced out the window. It was 6:17 AM and still dark. Sunrise at the Coast Guard Air Station at Floyd Bennett Field in Brooklyn, New York would come at 8:20 AM, but they knew the snow and sleet would keep the sky dark.

"Let's find out what happened," said Erickson as he walked off in the direction of the radio room.

The duty radioman looked up as Erickson and Bolton walked in.

"Any word on what caused the explosion?" asked Erickson.

"Yes, Sir," replied the radioman. "District Office just called. It's the USS *Turner.* She's been on Atlantic Patrol for nine months. She returned early this morning and anchored 4 miles SE of Rockaway Point, Long Island. A few minutes ago she had an explosion onboard and started burning. Coxswain Williams, at Coast Guard Sandy Hook, New Jersey, saw the explosion through the haze. Several 83 footers have been sent to the scene. The injured are being taken to the Army hospital at Fort Hancock on Sandy Hook. "

"Very well," said CDR Erickson. He looked at the calendar. It was January 3rd, 1944. "Keep me informed."

CDR Erickson was the commanding officer of the Coast Guard's first helicopter unit. He loved to fly and was an expert with the Sikorsky HNS-1 helicopter. LT Bolton, in contrast, had earned his helicopter wings just three days before.

CDR Erickson considered his HNS-1 helicopter. Its body was 33 feet long, its rotor wingspan was 38 inches, its engine had 200 horsepower, and it could fly over 65 miles per hour. The fabric-covered aluminum frame appeared flimsy, yet the helicopter had the ability to fly in nasty weather that would ground regular airplanes.

His mind went back to the fall of 1941 when he first read an article about a new invention called the helicopter. He immediately understood that the helicopter's ability to hover over one spot and to pick up people would make it a very practical and effective search and rescue tool. Then months later, Erickson met Igor Sikorsky, the inventor of the helicopter, watched a helicopter demonstration, and, after three hours of lessons, became Coast Guard Helicopter Pilot No.1. He just spent the past seven months starting a helicopter pilot training program and testing and proving the ability of the helicopter to land on and take off from ships.

BOOM! Again the doors shuddered and the windows rattled as the shock wave from a second larger explosion thudded against the building.

"No ship can survive that," he thought.

He knew that the wind, snow, and sleet outside had grounded all aircraft in the area. He also knew that, due to its design, the HNS-1 helicopter could fly in this weather.

"That's another reason the helicopter will replace the airplane as the Coast Guard's primary rescue aircraft," he said to himself.

The radioman at his office door interrupted his thoughts.

"Sir, the *Turner* just blew up, capsized, and sank. The crew abandoned ship, and Coast Guard units have rescued about half of them. The Post Hospital at Fort Hancock is overwhelmed with the injured."

CDR Erickson looked at his watch again. The dial read 8:00 AM. The sky had lightened with the approaching dawn, but the wind was still blowing 20-25 knots, and snow and sleet filled the air.

The phone rang. Erickson answered it.

"CDR Erickson? This is Admiral Parker," said the 3rd District Commander. "I know you are aware of the explosions and sinking of the *Turner.* Fort Hancock is treating 55 sailors and is running out of blood plasma. They have asked for help in getting plasma to them. All regular airplanes are grounded, and a car will take too long. Will your helicopter fly in this weather? I can get 40 units of blood plasma to Battery Park. Can you pick them up and fly them to Fort Hancock?"

CDR Erickson knew the HNS-1 could handle the weather, that this was a chance to prove the helicopter's capability, and that sailors would die if he didn't fly.

Yes, Sir!" Erickson said firmly.

Erickson, Bolton, and their crew rolled the HNS-1 out of the hanger, fired up the engine, got the rotor blades turning, and took off in a northerly direction for Battery Park.

Almost immediately, the helicopter disappeared in the "swirling snow whipped by gusting winds." (Beard, page 49)   Erickson worked hard to control the helicopter as wind gusts tried to knock the light aircraft off its course on the three mile flight. Snow and sleet covered the windshield, so Erickson relied upon his compass and followed his course until they could see the buildings and lights of lower Manhattan through the side windows.

He flew a high approach to stay clear of the pilings and landed the HNS-1. While LT Bolton hopped out and helped tie the two cases of blood plasma to the helicopter's floats, CDR Erickson countered the gusts by "flying" the helicopter in place on the ground. Erickson then realized that the blood plasma and LT Bolton were too much weight for the helo to carry. He ordered Bolton to remain at Battery Park.

"Aye, Aye, Sir," said Bolton reluctantly, but then added, "Sir, remember we landed with trees ahead of us, so you won't be able to take off into the wind."

"Looks like I'll have to back her out, then," Erickson replied as he gripped the controls, worked the pedals, and brought the aircraft to a hover. He carefully climbed, backed out over the pilings, and pivoted the helicopter. This time the wind pushed the helicopter as Erickson flew downwind due south to Fort Hancock on Sandy Hook. Hospital staff waited for him in the parking lot. The helicopter's rotor wash kicked up a snow cloud that covered the staff and made them look like snowmen. Within minutes the blood plasma was inside the hospital saving the lives of the injured crewmen.

With his fifteen minute errand of mercy completed, Erickson flew back to Battery Park for LT Bolton and then over to Air Station Brooklyn.

As they rolled the helicopter into the hanger, they realized the flight had set two records. They were the first pilots to fly a helicopter in such lousy weather, and this was the first time a helicopter had been used to save lives.

Chapter 2 - *Coast Guard Hero*

LCDR Richard Cammack Beyer leaned back in his chair, looked at his family around the supper table, and finished his story.

"Erickson's historic flight proved the helicopter could be a very valuable Coast Guard tool. His work with helicopters has also resulted in the rescue of hundreds of thousands of people since January 1944. As a Coast Guard aviator and helicopter pilot, I am following in Erickson's footsteps."

"Wow!" exclaimed David, his oldest son.

"Man!" said David's friend, Trevor, who was there for a sleepover.

"That's the best Coast Guard Hero story you have told us," said Lori, his wife.

"Sure is," chimed in Lindsay and Brad, the youngest two in the family.

"Thanks," said LCDR Beyer. "I'm glad the boys were making model airplanes when I got home from duty. David's plane reminded me of Erickson's first airplane, and Trevor's HH-65 Dolphin is the helicopter I fly."

"So you tell Coast Guard Hero stories, too. I thought only my Dad did that," Trevor said, thinking about his dad who was a chief boatswain's mate in the Coast Guard and an officer in charge of the United States Coast Guard Cutter (USCGC) *Bonita*.

"I thought I was the only one who told them," LCDR Beyer said. "I'll have to compare notes with your dad."

After the supper table was cleared and the kitchen cleaned, LCDR Beyer joined David and Trevor in the living room at their model making table.

David looked up from painting the wing of his model. "Dad, you said that my model airplane reminded you of Erickson's plane. How was that?"

"That's a Fokker PJ," his dad replied, "and that was the kind of plane Erickson commanded when he flew his first rescue mission back in 1936."

Chapter 3 - *Arcturus Rescue*

LT Erickson sat in the ready room at Air Station Miami. It was January 7, 1936. Six months earlier he graduated from flight school and earned his wings as Aviator No. 32. *Arcturus*, a Fokker PJ, was his plane and he was its pilot. The PJ had been specifically designed and built for the USCG. It had a boat shaped fuselage so it could land on water and a front hatch so crewmen could pull people out of the water or life rafts to safety.

Suddenly, the station alarm bell rang. Erickson jumped to his feet and raced to *Arcturus*. His co-pilot and air crew joined him, and they climbed into the PJ and started its engines. The sun was out, the sky was clear, and the wind was light.

The control tower gave Erickson his orders. "A 30-foot cabin cruiser has not returned to port from a day trip in the ocean. Find it!" Erickson pushed the throttles forward. The whine of the propellers increased to a high pitch, and *Arcturus* gained speed, lifted off the water and into the air.

Erickson flew to the southwest until he was near the last known position of the boat. He started a search pattern that took them down the boat's drift path. This gave the aircrew the best possible chance to spot the boat.

Their search pattern took them over Rebecca's Shoals in the Gulf of Mexico.

"I see a boat, port side," a crewman called out over the intercom system.

Erickson flew low over the boat.

"It must be them," said the co-pilot. "There are people on deck waving white rags."

While flying over the boat, Erickson looked at the water and verified the height and direction of the waves as well as the wind speed. He confirmed it was safe to land.

"Let's put her down," said Erickson. He landed *Arcturus* on the water and taxied over to the boat. "Tell me what you see, Chief," he ordered.

The crew chief boarded the boat, looked around, went below decks, and returned to *Arcturus*. He reported to Erikson, "Sir, there are seven passengers who are tired, hungry, dehydrated, and sunburned. Their motor pump failed which caused the engine to stop. They lost their anchor and have been drifting for 30 hours."

"Bring them aboard, Chief, and tend to the injured ones," Erickson said.

"Aye, Aye, Sir," was his reply, and the survivors were loaded into *Arcturus*.

LT Erickson revved the engines, pointed the plane into the wind and waves, and took off. He flew to the northeast, back to Air Station Miami and medical care.

Ground crews carefully helped the boaters out and placed them in ambulances that took them to the hospital for observation and treatment.

LT Erickson walked back to the ready room to await the next emergency.

"So he saved seven lives?" asked Trevor.

"Yes," said LCDR Beyer. "Everyone survived."

Chapter 4 - *Beginnings*

"How did CAPT Erickson become interested in flying?" asked Trevor.

"Erickson was at the Coast Guard Academy," LCDR Beyer explained, "when he witnessed an event which convinced him to become a pilot."

"What happened, Dad?" David asked.

"Back in 1928, the Coast Guard flew airplanes that could land on water and then taxi around like a boat," LCDR Beyer explained. "One of these planes flew to the Academy to give a demonstration. The pilot landed on the Thames River near the Academy and then hit a yacht. Cadet Erickson saw the plane as it was winched onto the shore for repairs. He had never seen an airplane so close before, and was fascinated by its boat-shaped fuselage and the curve of its wings. He decided then and there that he wanted to be a pilot."

"Why did planes land on the water?" Lindsay asked.

"When the airplane first became popular, cities did not have runways or airports and they were very expensive to build. However, most cities had rivers, lakes, or oceans near them and these became inexpensive, ready-made runways. So planes were designed with boat bottoms so they could use the water as a runway."

He continued, "The ability to land on water was very important to the Coast Guard. Float planes had the speed to fly quickly out to a cargo ship to rescue a hurt sailor or to find a lost boat. Once on scene, the boat hull allowed the plane to land on the water, taxi to the boat or cargo ship, and rescue the boater or sailor. If a person was seriously hurt, the plane could fly them quickly back to base where an ambulance would take them to the hospital."

"Dad?" asked David. "Isn't the Coast Guard Academy in New London, Connecticut?"

"It is now," said his father. "But when Erickson graduated, it was at nearby Fort Trumbull. The Academy is the USCG's military college that trains and educates its officers. Erikson graduated in 1931."

"What year did you graduate, Mr. Beyer?" asked Trevor.

"In the year 2000," said LCDR Beyer. "Erickson went to flight school after a tour of duty on the USCGC *Chelan*. He earned his wings and graduated in July 1935 as Coast Guard Aviator No. 32. At that time, the Coast Guard had only 13 airplanes and 13 aviators, and the helicopter had not been invented."

"How many do you have now?" asked David.

"We have over 200 aircraft and more than 800 aviators on active duty," responded LCDR Beyer. They fly four types of airplanes and two types of helicopters."

Mrs. Beyer joined them in the living room with a tray of sugar cookies. Anticipating the boy's next question, she jumped into the conversation. "David, your father graduated from flight school in 2004 and is Coast Guard Aviator No. 3658."

"How do you know that, Mom?" asked Lindsay while munching on a cookie.

"Easy Peasy, Lindsay," she replied. "I met your father while he was at flight school in 2004. He let me pin on his wings when he graduated. Then he got down on one knee and asked me to marry him. I said yes."

USCG Academy, Fort Trumbuli

"What happened next?" Brad, the youngest, asked impatiently.

"We got married," said his father with a smile.

Brad scowled and whined, "Daaaad! I mean about CAPT Erickson!"

Chapter 5 - *Pearl Harbor*

"Our story jumps to August 1941 and the Naval Air Station at Ford Island in Pearl Harbor, Hawaii," continued LCDR Beyer. "LT Erickson had been a pilot for five years and was an experienced aviator. He commanded a plane at Oakland, California and flew from the cutters *Hamilton* and *Duane* in Alaska during Bering Sea patrols."

David interrupted. "How do you fly a plane from a cutter, Dad? They don't have a flight deck."

"Good point," his father said. "The planes were strapped on to the fantail of the cutter. When a mission needed to be flown, a crane lowered the plane into the water and the pilot used the ocean as a runway. When the mission was finished, the crane hoisted the plane back onto the cutter where it was stored on the fantail until it was needed again.

"It was at Pearl Harbor, while assigned to the USCGC *Taney*, that Erickson read an article about a new rotary-wing machine called the helicopter. It was built by Dr. Igor Sikorsky.

"Erickson immediately recognized that the helicopter's ability to hover in one spot and pick up a person would make it an excellent search and rescue tool."

"Well, he was right," said Trevor. "My dad says helos hoist people off the *Bonita* all the time."

"We sure do," said LCDR Beyer, "and the hoist we use today was invented by CAPT Erickson, but we are getting ahead of ourselves.

"Without warning, the Japanese attacked Pearl Harbor and Erickson found himself in the middle of the battle, surrounded by 1,500 men needing rescue, and no way to do it."

Chapter 6 - *Surprise Attack*

"It's going to be another beautiful Hawaiian day," LT Erickson thought.

It was Sunday, December 7, 1941. The sky was blue, the air was clear, and the temperature was mild. He was in the Administration Building at the Naval Air Station (NAS) on Ford Island and ready to go home after a night's duty. His relief had arrived, and they watched the Marine Corps color guard march to the flag pole.

"Everything all set for colors?" he asked as he stepped inside the building. The answer was drowned out by two heavy explosions outside. Running to the door, Erickson looked out in time to see an airplane fly over the Navy Yard and drop a torpedo. He saw a red rising sun painted on each wing. "The Japanese are attacking," he thought. Then the torpedo exploded against the bow of the USS *California*, and he ducked back inside.

The base public address system sounded General Quarters (GQ). The phone rang. Erickson answered.

"What the hell kind of drills are you pulling down there?" shouted CAPT James M. Shoemaker, the NAS Commanding Officer. Erickson explained. Within minutes the Captain arrived and assumed command, leaving Erickson to go to his GQ station.

Erickson stepped outside. Thudding sounds halted him. Bullet, bomb, and shell fragments were slamming into the ground and bouncing off the runway. It was raining shrapnel. Erickson ducked back inside. He collected his thoughts, took a deep breath, lowered his head, and sprinted to the land plane control tower and his GQ station.

He took charge of the machine gun battery, which was being set up on the roof of the operations building, and found himself with a birds-eye view of the entire attack. He ducked as waves of attacking aircraft flew past, saw planes burning on the runway, and cringed when the USS *Arizona* blew up. To his horror, a burning oil slick spread across the harbor and engulfed battleship row. Sailors trapped on burning ships had no way to be rescued. They could only jump into the burning waters and try to swim underwater to safety. Erickson looked on in frustration as sailors struggled and died in the burning oil coated waters.

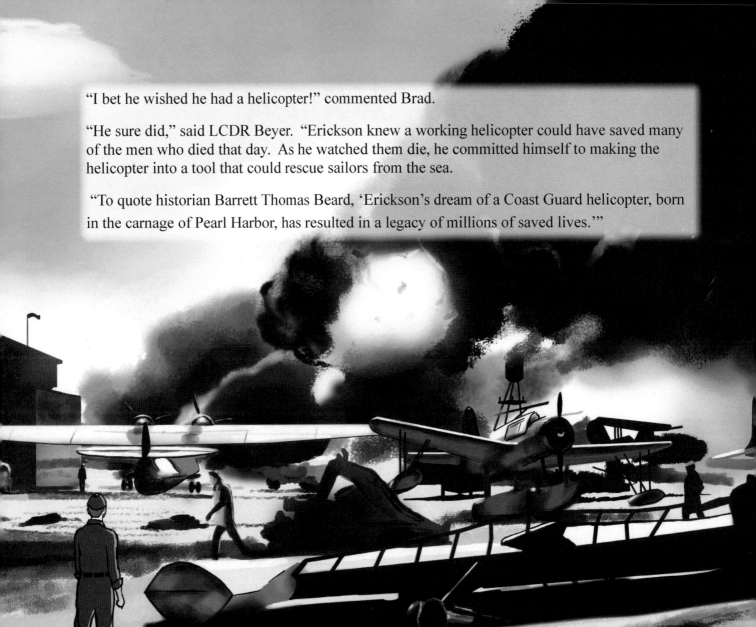

"I bet he wished he had a helicopter!" commented Brad.

"He sure did," said LCDR Beyer. "Erickson knew a working helicopter could have saved many of the men who died that day. As he watched them die, he committed himself to making the helicopter into a tool that could rescue sailors from the sea.

"To quote historian Barrett Thomas Beard, 'Erickson's dream of a Coast Guard helicopter, born in the carnage of Pearl Harbor, has resulted in a legacy of millions of saved lives.'"

Chapter 7 - *Sikorsky's Helicopter*

"It seems to me he was very successful," said Mrs. Beyer. "How did he do it?"

"He did it with lots of hard work and perseverance," replied her husband. "Erickson's first step was to get reassigned to the East Coast so he could be near the Sikorsky Helicopter plant in Bridgeport, Connecticut. His promotion to Lieutenant Commander (LCDR) meant getting a new assignment, so Erickson requested and received orders to Coast Guard Air Station Brooklyn at Floyd Bennett Field. He was the executive officer, and now only 65 miles from Bridgeport.

"On June 26, 1942, Erickson, as a favor, flew LT Healy to Bridgeport. The officer was meeting with Igor Sikorsky and thought Erickson might like to meet him. The two hit it off right away, and Sikorsky personally demonstrated the helicopter's ability to hover and land within inches of a specific spot. Any doubts Erickson may have had about the helicopter vanished. Erickson visited the Sikorsky factory regularly and discussed helicopter ideas with the engineers. He arranged for senior officers to see helicopter demonstrations. Then, because Erickson was already so involved with helicopters, Captain Kossler, LT Healy's boss and head of the Coast Guard helicopter program, picked Erickson to be the Coast Guard's first helicopter pilot. After only three hours of instruction, Erickson flew solo, making him Coast Guard Helicopter Pilot No. 1."

"Impressive!" commented David.

"Erickson formed and led the Coast Guard's first helicopter detachment at Coast Guard Air Station Brooklyn," LCDR Beyer went on.

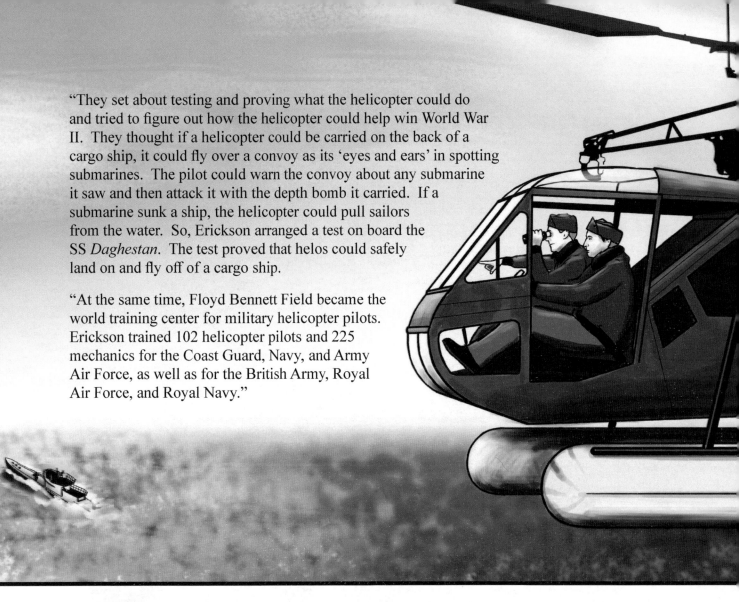

"They set about testing and proving what the helicopter could do and tried to figure out how the helicopter could help win World War II. They thought if a helicopter could be carried on the back of a cargo ship, it could fly over a convoy as its 'eyes and ears' in spotting submarines. The pilot could warn the convoy about any submarine it saw and then attack it with the depth bomb it carried. If a submarine sunk a ship, the helicopter could pull sailors from the water. So, Erickson arranged a test on board the SS *Daghestan*. The test proved that helos could safely land on and fly off of a cargo ship.

"At the same time, Floyd Bennett Field became the world training center for military helicopter pilots. Erickson trained 102 helicopter pilots and 225 mechanics for the Coast Guard, Navy, and Army Air Force, as well as for the British Army, Royal Air Force, and Royal Navy."

He continued. "Erickson did such a good job training pilots that the King of England, King George VI, gave him the Award of Honorary Member of the Military Division of the Most Excellent Order of the British Empire – in other words, he made him a Knight."

"Sir Frank!" exclaimed Brad while performing a deep bow.

Chapter 8 - *Proving It Works*

"CDR Erickson was convinced that the helicopter, when improved, would eventually become the Coast Guard's primary rescue aircraft," LCDR Beyer went on. "He worked tirelessly to improve it. He knew a power hoist and rescue slings would be needed to lift sailors out of the sea, so he made them. He then made them better and better until they were practical pieces of equipment. He invented inflatable pontoons so the HNS-1 could land on water or soft ground.

"Almost every day he proved the helicopter's ability to do things that other aircraft could not. His Life Flight in January 1944 proved the helicopter could fly safely in bad weather. In August 1944, he proved a helicopter could lift sailors out of the water. Erickson became the first helicopter pilot to pick up a man, pick up a man floating on the water, and pick up a man from a life raft."

LCDR Beyer continued. "The combination of the hydraulic hoist and sling he invented and the lifesaving methods he developed convinced the US Army that helicopters could be safely used to lift and fly soldiers, equipment, and cargo. It sent helicopters overseas to rescue hurt soldiers.

"In April of 1945, he became the Chief of the Research and Development Office. He could now work full-time testing and developing helicopters. He helped create rules for helicopter-shipboard operations, and was involved with tests held on board the USCG-manned USS *Cobb*.

"He also discovered that helicopters, with their ability to fly in the confined space of the harbor and hover if necessary, were ideal for helping ships in port to calibrate their gun control radar systems. The high demand for radar sighting missions kept Erickson and other helicopter pilots in the air, giving them as much flight time as they needed.

"In April, 1945, though remaining at the Brooklyn air station, he was relieved of his command so that he could devote full-time to testing and developing the use of helicopters with the title of Chief, Research and Development Office. He was involved with official demonstrations held on board the USCG-manned USS Cobb (WPG-181), which was being used as the testing platform for helicopter-shipboard operations."

Chapter 9 - *Sabena DC-4 Crash*

"Disassemble your helicopter and have it ready for C-54 transport this evening!" ordered Captain Richard Burke, the Coast Guard's Eastern Area Rescue Officer, "And get CDR Erickson back to Elizabeth City to take charge!"

"Yes, Sir!" replied LT Stewart Graham, Coast Guard Aviator No. 144 and Helicopter Pilot No. 2, as he glanced at his watch. It was 2:45 on the afternoon of 20 September 1946. He had less than 7 hours' time to do this, and CDR Erickson was in New York City.

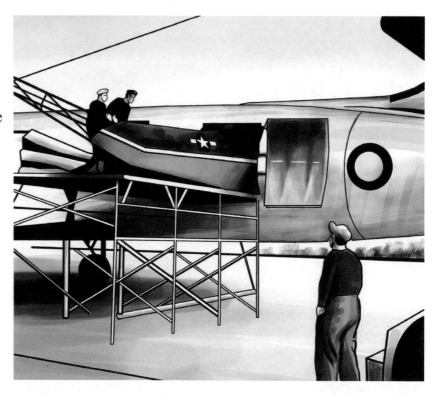

Graham ran into the hanger and grabbed his chief aircraft mechanic. "We've got a downed commercial airliner in Newfoundland with survivors. We are going to airlift the helos to Gander and rescue them. Start taking the HNS-1 apart, pick a crew to go with you, and gather all the tools and spare parts you will need."

"Good work, LT Graham," said CDR Erickson through the phone, after LT Graham had contacted him in New York and told him of his preparations.

"This is going to be a lot like the Labrador rescue we did last year. I'll fly back right away. I can be there by 7 PM. Tell me what happened."

27

"Two days ago," LT Graham began, "a Sabena DC-4 crashed on approach to the airport in Gander, Newfoundland. Yesterday, the crash site was located. Supplies have been dropped and a rescue team of Newfoundland woodsmen and Army personnel is hiking through the woods to aid the survivors. There is no room for planes to land. Helicopters are the only hope to get anyone out alive. The Coast Guard has two available; the Bell HOS-1 at Brooklyn and our HNS-1 here in Elizabeth City."

Erickson hung up, rushed to his plane, and returned to Coast Guard Air Station Elizabeth City in North Carolina where he had been reassigned in June of 1946. He realized this mission would be very important to the acceptance of the helicopter because it would be the first time helicopters would be used in a major civilian rescue. This was a chance to prove the helicopter's amazing capabilities to a watching world.

Erickson arrived to find their helicopter disassembled, the spare parts assembled, and the crew waiting. The C-54 arrived and loading began. By 11:45 PM, less than nine hours after LT Graham answered the phone, they were wheels up on their way to Gander.

A report came in from Captain Samuel P. Martin, the U.S. Army medical doctor in the search party, which confirmed the need for their helicopters.

 "18 survivors…14 stretcher cases…4 ambulatory...26 dead. Condition of the injured demands immediate hospitalization... Suggest evacuation via helicopter, due to the remoteness and impenetrability of the terrain."

Their C-54 landed at Gander airport at 6:25 AM and taxied to the hangar. Chief Aviation Machinist's Mate Vanelli began unloading Brooklyn's HOS-1 with Gander's only crane. The four pilots, CDR Erickson, LT Graham, LT Kleisch, and LT Bolton, took off in a PBY Catalina Flying Boat to over-fly the crash site and to map an evacuation route. The pilots selected a landing site in a grassy area on top of the mountain close to the wreckage. They agreed the fastest evacuation method was to fly the survivors 12 miles to the edge of Lake Gander and transfer them to PBYs that could fly them quickly to Gander airport and medical help.

CDR Erickson realized the helicopters would sink into the soggy Muskeg that covered the area and ordered wooden landing platforms built at each site. PBYs dropped the lumber, and platforms soon appeared.

"CDR Erickson?" Chief Vanelli said. "The HOS-1 is ready. The HNS-1 will be ready soon."

Erickson looked at his watch. It was 2:30 PM.

"Chief, that's phenomenal," exclaimed CDR Erickson. "Less than 24 hours ago we were in the States and now we are operational in Newfoundland. On top of that, you put the HOS-1 together in only 4 and 1/2 hours. Incredible!"

He turned to LT Kleisch. "Take off and start hauling survivors. You will have a PBY flying cover in case anything goes wrong."

LT Kleisch reached the crash site in 27 minutes, took on his first survivor, and flew to Lake Gander. The survivor was transferred to a rubber raft, towed out to the PBY, transferred again to the PBY, and flown to Gander airport. The first round trip took an hour and a half. The second took only 20 minutes as wrinkles were ironed out. LT Kleisch flew out the eighth survivor at sunset, and flew back to Gander airport in the dark.

The next morning both helicopters were ready. The pilots flew repeat trips between the crash site and Lake Gander to bring out the ten remaining survivors. Then they ferried out the fourteen US Army rescuers who had hiked in to the site. On the third day they flew investigators and a representative of Sabena Airlines to the wreckage. The flight back to Gander airport, the 40th flight of the rescue, successfully ended the Coast Guard's first-of-a-kind major rescue operation.

CDR Erickson wrapped up the operation by thanking the crews. "You have truly done an outstanding job," he said. "In less than 24 hours from notification, we were operational in Newfoundland and had rescued eight survivors. Darkness prevented further rescue. At first light you were back in the air and brought out the ten remaining survivors as well as the fourteen people in the rescue party. Everyone was rescued in less than 48 hours.

"Some of you didn't sleep the entire time, and Chief Vanelli and his team probably set a recorded in putting the HOS-1 back together in 4 and 1/2 hours. I know we all did what we had signed up to do and had been trained to do, but without your extreme dedication to duty, this would not have happened as well as it did."

He continued. "The newspapers will call this a miracle, but LT Kleisch reminded me that this rescue is a fine example of inter-service and civilian teamwork and proper coordination of manpower and equipment. Eighteen people, who would have died, are alive today because of teamwork, coordination, and our helicopters."

The Coast Guard recognized CDR Erickson and his aircrew's outstanding success by awarding them the Air Medal. The Belgian government awarded each member of the team a commission as a "Knight of the Order of Leopold."

Chapter 10 - *Semper Paratus (Always Ready)*

"That was the beginning of the end of the Coast Guard's resistance to helicopters," said LCDR Beyer. "Erickson's vision of the helicopter as the Coast Guard's primary search and rescue tool was becoming a reality."

"Pretty cool, Dad," said Lindsay. "Was the Hurricane Katrina rescue a bit like Gander?"

"Yes, it was," replied his father. "It is the Coast Guard's biggest rescue operation so far and proved Erickson was right. We flew 1,817 sorties and rescued 12,535 people. I was very proud to be a part of it.

"The Gander crash and rescue created world-wide publicity, and the Coast Guard was deluged with requests for helo presentations and demonstrations. Dignitaries would show up at Elizabeth City and ask for a ride. LT Graham flew as many demonstrations as he could because CAPT Erickson knew every ride would convince one more person that the helicopter was versatile and therefore valuable for search and rescue."

David held up the model he had been working on. "All done," he said.

"So is my story," said LCDR Beyer as he sat down.

Trevor showed off his helicopter. "Same here," he said.

"Good work, boys," said LCDR Beyer. "Now, time to head up to bed."

Mrs. Beyer spoke seriously. "Erickson was a dedicated officer and a good pilot," she said.

"He sure was," said LCDR Beyer quietly. "I feel fortunate to be following in his footsteps."

Changing her tone, she looked at David and Trevor who were delaying their departure. "Boys, you heard the Commander," she said. "Fly those aircraft upstairs and get ready for bed."

"Aye, aye, Ma'am," they said in unison as they stood up, saluted, and flew towards the stairs.

"Thanks for the story, Dad," said David over his shoulder,

"Yeah, thanks, Mr. Beyer," said Trevor

"Semper Paratus, boys," said LCDR Beyer.

"Semper Paratus," they shouted back as they disappeared up the stairs in search of people to rescue.

Commander Frank A. Erickson, USCG

Appendix A

Timeline of Captain Frank A. Erickson, USCG

1907-1978

6 November 1907 - Born at Tillamook, OR, and raised in Portland, OR.

1925 - Enlisted in the U.S. Navy.

1927 - Received U.S. Naval Academy appointment.

15 June 1927 - Reported to U.S. Naval Academy, Annapolis, MD.

7 February 1928 - Resigned U.S. Naval Academy appointment.

26 April 1928 - Enlisted in U.S. Coast Guard. Attended Boot Camp and ordered to the USCGC *Algonquin* in the Northwestern Division.

11 August 1928 - Received appointment to U.S. Coast Guard Academy (Fort Trumbull).

June 1930 - Interest in aviation began when he witnessed a damaged Coast Guard plane being dragged from the Thames River onto the beach for repairs. The plane had an unavoidable collision with the yacht *Minx* at the New London boat races.

15 May 1931 - Graduated and commissioned an Ensign. Served three years sea duty on USCGC *Chelan* based out of Seattle, WA as assistant navigator and assistant engineer. Applied for flight training.

1 April 1934 – Assigned as flight student at U.S. Naval Air Station, Pensacola, FL.

July 1935 - Earned wings. Designated Coast Guard Aviator No. 32. Assigned U.S. Coast Guard Air Station Miami, Fl.

7 January 1936 - Piloted Fokker PJ *Arcturus* in rescuing seven persons on board V-2395 adrift near Rebecca's Shoals in the Gulf of Mexico. The 30-foot cabin cruiser, enroute to Fort Jefferson, Dry Tortugas Island, experienced motor pump failure and lost its anchor. The boat drifted for 30 hours and several persons suffered from exposure.

March 1938 - Assigned U.S. Coast Guard Air Station San Diego, CA and in command of a plane attached to Coast Guard Base Eleven at Oakland, CA.

1938 Bering Sea Patrol - Temporary duty as pilot of plane attached to USCGC *Hamilton*.

1939 Bering Sea Patrol - Temporary duty as pilot of plane attached to USCGC *Duane*.

August 1939 - Piloted Grumman JRF-2 attached to USCGC *Taney* at Pearl Harbor.

January 1941 - Assigned to U.S. Coast Guard district office in Honolulu.

7 December 1941 – Witnessed Japanese attack on Pearl Harbor. He was just coming off duty as the watch officer on Ford Island when the Japanese attacked.

May 1942 - Promoted to Lieutenant Commander (LCDR) and transferred to U.S. Coast Guard Air Station Brooklyn, NY at Floyd Bennett Field

26 June 1942 - LCDR Erickson flies LT Healy to Bridgeport, CT to inspect the VS-300 helicopter and meet Igor I. Sikorsky.

29 June 1942 - Sends memo from the Sikorsky plant recommending the helicopter as ideal for lifesaving, for law enforcement patrols, and for being the "eyes and ears" of convoy escorts in spotting submarines. Insists helicopters could be carried on any ship that had a suitable landing platform.

19 February 1943 - ADM Ernest J. King, USN placed "the responsibility for the seagoing development of the helicopter with the U.S. Coast Guard" and began the U.S. Coast Guard's role in developing the helicopter for use in a variety of applications.

April 1943 - Ordered to the Sikorsky Aircraft plant at Bridgeport, Connecticut to become a helicopter pilot, establish liaison with the manufacturer, and learn about the construction and operation of helicopters. Completed Sikorsky training and designated as an instructor and as Coast Guard Helicopter Pilot No. 1.

7 May 1943 - Helicopter trials take place aboard the SS *Bunker Hill*, proving helicopter can safely land on and take off from cargo ships.

June 1943 - Makes several observations. Helicopters 1) could fly in low visibility and low ceiling weather that would ground fixed-wing aircraft, 2) could land on small platforms, and 3) would be more effective as the "eyes and ears" of a convoy in finding enemy submarines than they would be as "killer aircraft" in sinking the submarine.

38

July 1943 - Formed the first Coast Guard Helicopter Detachment at U.S Coast Guard Air Station Brooklyn with two other officers and five aviation machinist mates.

19 November 1943 - Navy sends three HNS-1 helicopters to Floyd Bennett Field to be used to start a helicopter pilot training program under the direction of LCDR Erickson.

November 1943 - Joint U.S.-British evaluation trials held on board the SS *Daghestan* to determine the limiting conditions for carrying out helicopter flights from a ship underway at sea.

1 December 1943 - Promoted to Commander (CDR).

3 January 1944 - Conducted first helicopter lifesaving flight. Piloted an HNS-1, with two cases of blood plasma lashed to its floats, from New York City to army post hospital at Fort Hancock in Sandy Hook, NJ. Plasma saved lives of numerous Navy crewmen from the destroyer USS *Turner*, which exploded, burned, capsized, and sank that morning off New York harbor. Performed this heroic deed in violent winds and snow that grounded all other aircraft. First pilot in the world to fly a helicopter under such conditions.

May 1944 - Assigned Commanding Officer, Air Station Brooklyn.

June 1944 - Helicopter school at Floyd Bennett Field begins training pilots and mechanics. In the next two years, Erickson trains 102 helicopter pilots and 225 mechanics for the U.S. Army Air Force and Navy and the British Army, Royal Air Force, and Navy, as well as the USCG. King George VI rewards Erickson's service by making him an Honorary Member of the Military Division of the Most Excellent Order of the British Empire. The citation specifically cited Erickson's assistance "in the development of the British helicopter flying training at the Floyd Bennett Field, and it was largely due to his kindness and magnificent co-operation that this training achieved such excellent results."

11 August 1944 - First helicopter pickup of a man.

14 August 1944 - First helicopter pickup of a man floating in water.

25 September 1944 - First helicopter pickup of a man from a life-raft.

February 1945 - Awarded official commendation for helicopter demonstrations.

April 1945 - Assigned as Chief, Research and Development Office and devoted full-time to developing and testing the helicopter. Involved with official demonstrations on board the Coast Guard manned USS *Cobb*, being used as the testing platform for helicopter-shipboard operations.

27 April 1945 - Led effort to rescue Royal Canadian Air Force crew whose plane had crashed in Labrador. Disassembled one Coast Guard helicopter, transported it by aircraft to Goose Bay, and re-assembled it. LT Kleisch safely rescued 9 survivors.

June 1946 - Transferred to CG Air Station Elizabeth City, NC where he established the Rotary Wing Development Unit.

18 September 1946 - Led effort to rescue crew of Belgian Sabena DC-4 airliner that crashed in Newfoundland. Disassembled two Coast Guard helicopters, transported them by aircraft to Newfoundland, re-assembled them, and safely rescued 18 survivors. Awarded U.S. Air Medal and commissioned by Belgium as a "Knight of the Order of Leopold."

April 1950 - Promoted to Captain and assigned as CG Liaison Officer at the U.S Naval Air Test Center, Patuxent River, MD.

27 January 1951 - Graduated from U.S. Navy Test Pilot School. Assigned as Assistant to the Chief of the Aviation Division, CG Headquarters. Appointed member of the National Advisory Committee for Aeronautics' Committee on Helicopters.

1952 - Appointed to the National Advisory Committee for Aeronautics' Committee on Helicopters.

July 1952 - Assigned to the Civil Aeronautics Administration in Washington, D.C.

1953 - Appointed to the National Advisory Committee for Aeronautics' Committee on Helicopters.

January 1953, Assigned as Chief of the Search and Rescue Section, Operations Division, Third Coast Guard District Office (NYC).

1 July 1954 - Retired from U.S. Coast Guard. Became Chief Test Pilot for Brantly Helicopter Corporation. Continued to design helicopter flight-path stabilizer. Assisted NASA's Gemini program in developing a hoist system to lift an astronaut out of the water. Helped design flight deck for USCG's 210-foot Reliance Class cutters.

17 December 1978 - Crossed the bar.

Past and Present USCG Aircraft
<u>Loening OL Amphibian</u>

The **Loening OL** was an American two-seat amphibious biplane built by Loening for the U.S. Army Air Corps and the U.S. Navy. The Coast Guard purchased three Loening OL-5 amphibians in October 1926, soon after Congress appropriated $152,000 to establish a permanent Coast Guard aviation detachment. These three amphibians, along with two Chance-Vought UO-4's, were the first aircraft purchased by the Coast Guard, and their purchase marks the true "beginning" of Coast Guard aviation.

General characteristics

- **Crew:** two   **Length:** 34 ft 9 in
- **Wingspan:** 45 ft 0 in   **Height:** 12 ft 9 in
- **Wing area:** 504 ft2   **Empty weight:** 3649 lb
- **Gross weight:** 5404 lb
- **Powerplant:** 1 × <u>Pratt & Whitney R-1340-4</u> Wasp radial piston engine, 450 hp

Performance

- **Maximum speed:** 122 mph
- **Range:** 625 miles
- **Service ceiling:** 14,300 ft

Fokker PJ Flying Boat

The **Fokker PJ** was a flying boat built by Fokker's American operation in 1930 specifically for the Coast Guard as a search-and-rescue aircraft. Fokker was purchased by General Motors in 1930 and renamed General Aviation. The PJ was a high-wing cantilever monoplane with a flying boat hull and outrigger pontoons mounted on the wings. Twin pusher engines were mounted on pylons above the wings. The hull was metal, and the wing was wood covered with plywood. The PJ had both a boat hull and retractable landing gear so it was able to land on both water and land. The USCG's five PJs were named *Antares, Altair, Acrux, Acamar,* and *Arcturus.*

General characteristics
- **Crew:** Four - Pilots (2), Nav, Radio
- **Wingspan:** 74 ft 2 in
- **Wing area:** 754 ft2
- **Gross weight:** 11,200 lb
- **Powerplant:** 2 × Pratt & Whitney R-1340 Wasp radial piston engine, 420 hp ea

Length: 53 ft 9 in
Height: 15 ft 6 in
Empty weight: 7,000 lb

Performance
- **Maximum speed:** 130 mph
- **Range:** 1,100 miles
- **Service ceiling:** 9,000 ft

Grumman J2F Duck (Bering Sea)

The **Grumman J2F Duck** (company designation **G-15**) was an American single-engine amphibious biplane. It was used by each major branch of the U.S. armed forces from the mid-1930s until just after World War II, primarily for utility and air-sea rescue duties. It was also used by the Argentine Navy, who took delivery of their first Duck in 1937. After the war, J2F Ducks saw service with independent civilian operators, as well as the armed forces of Colombia and Mexico.

General characteristics

- **Crew:** two (pilot and observer)   **Capacity:** two rescued airmen
- **Length:** 34 ft 0 in   **Wingspan:** 39 ft 0 in
- **Height:** 13 ft 11 in   **Wing area:** 409 ft²
- **Empty weight:** 5,480 lb   **Loaded weight:** 7,700 lb
- **Powerplant:** 1 × Wright R-1820-54 nine-cylinder radial engine, 900 hp

Performance

- **Maximum speed:** 190 mph
- **Cruise speed:** 155 mph
- **Range:** 780 miles
- **Service ceiling:** 20,000 ft

Sikorsky HNS-1 Hoverfly

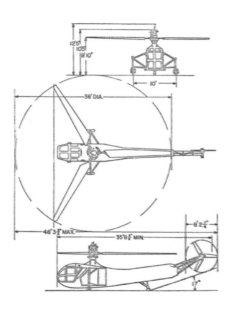

The world's first large-scale mass-produced helicopter was built for the Army by Igor Sikorsky and labeled the R-4 after the first three models (R-1, R-2, R-3) failed. The R-4 was a two-seat helicopter with a single, three-bladed, main rotor powered by a radial engine. The R-4 was the first helicopter used by the United States' Army Air Force, Navy, and Coast Guard and the United Kingdom's Royal Air Force and Navy. The helicopter was called the Sikorsky R-4 by the Army, HNS-1 by the U.S. Navy and Coast Guard, while the British called it the **Hoverfly**.

Endurance: 2 hours
Range: 130 miles
Top speed: 74 mph
Cruise speed: 65 mph
Rotor Diameter: 38 ft 1 in
Length: 48 ft 1 in
Engine type: Warner R-550-3 piston, 185 hp

Sikorsky HH-60 Black Hawk

The **Sikorsky MH-60T Jayhawk** is a multi-mission, twin-engine, medium-range helicopter operated by the United States Coast Guard for search and rescue, law enforcement, military readiness and marine environmental protection missions.

Range: 807.8 miles
Top speed: 207 mph
Wingspan: 54 ft 0 in
Length: 65 ft
Cruise speed: 162 mph
Unit cost: $17,000,000
Engine type: General Electric T700

Eurocopter HH-65 Dolphin

The **Eurocopter HH-65 Dolphin** is a twin-engine, single main rotor, MEDEVAC-capable search and rescue helicopter operated by the United States Coast Guard. It is a variant of the French-built Eurocopter AS365 Dauphin.

Range: 409 miles
Top speed: 135 mph
Wingspan: 39 ft 0 in
Length: 38 ft
Unit cost: $9,000,000
Engine type: Turbomeca Arriel
First flight: 1980

Lockheed Martin C-130J Super Hercules

The **Lockheed Martin C-130J Super Hercules** is a four-engine turboprop military transport aircraft. The C-130J is a comprehensive update of the Lockheed C-130 Hercules, with new engines, flight deck, and other systems.

Range: 3510 miles
Cruise speed: 355 mph
Wingspan: 133 ft 0 in
Unit cost: $70,370,000 (1996)
Engine type: Turboprop
Manufacturer: Lockheed Martin
First flight: April 5, 1996
Introduced: 1999

Appendix C

United States Coast Guard

Motto – Semper Paratus (Always Ready)

The Coast Guard is the nation's oldest continuous seagoing service with responsibilities for Search and Rescue (SAR), Maritime Law Enforcement (MLE), Aids to Navigation (ATON), Ice Breaking, Environmental Protection, Port Security and Military Readiness. AS a first responder and humanitarian service, the Coast Guard provides aid to people in distress or impacted by natural and man-made disasters whether at sea or ashore. Its over 56,000 members operate a multi-mission fleet of 243 Cutters, 201 fixed and rotary-wing aircraft, and over 1,600 boats. The Coast Guard protects and defends more than 100,000 miles of U.S. coastline. It is one of the five Armed Services of the United States and is the only military branch in the Department of Homeland Security

On an average day, the Coast Guard:
- Conducts 45 search and rescue cases;
- saves 10 lives;
- saves over $1.2M in property;
- seizes 874 pounds of cocaine and 214 pounds of marijuana;
- conducts 57 waterborne patrols of critical maritime infrastructure;
- interdicts 17 illegal migrants;
- escorts 5 high-capacity passenger vessels;
- conducts 24 security boardings in and around U.S. ports;
- screens 360 merchant vessels for potential security threats prior to arrival in U.S. ports;
- conducts 14 fisheries conservation boardings;
- services 82 buoys and fixed aids to navigation;
- investigates 35 pollution incidents;
- completes 26 safety examinations on foreign vessels;
- conducts 105 marine inspections;
- investigates 14 marine casualties involving commercial vessels;
- facilitates movement of $8.7B worth of goods and commodities through the Nation's Maritime Transportation System.

References and Sources

A great wealth of material was obtained for this book from internet searches for "CDR Erickson," "HNS-1," and "CG Aviation." Primary sources of material include:

"Complete history of CG Aviation," last modified January 12, 2017, http://uscgaviationhistory. aoptero.org/

"Sikorsky HNS-1 "Hoverfly," last modified December 21, 2016, https://www.uscg.mil/history/ aviationindex.asp - Source for Chapters 1-10.

"Captain Frank A. Erickson USCG," last modified December 21, 2016, https://www.uscg.mil/ history/aviationindex.asp - Source for Appendix A

"Average Coast Guard Day," last modified December 21, 2016, https://www.uscg.mil/budget/ average_day.asp- Source for Appendix C.

"The Coast Guard's Katrina Documentation Project," last modified December 21, 2016, https:// www.uscg.mil/history/katrina/docs/karthistory.asp - Source for back cover rescue statistics.

"Aviation Centennial," last modified January 12, 2017, http://centennial-cgaviation.org

Robert M. Browning Jr, *"The Eyes and Ears of the Convoy: Development of the helicopter as an anti-submarine weapon," Commandant's Bulletin,* September 1993.

Barrett Thomas Beard, *Wonderful Flying Machines: A History of U.S. Coast Guard Helicopters,* (Annapolis: Naval Institute Press, 1996). As I neared completion of this book, I discovered Barrett Thomas Beard had written a comprehensive account of Erickson's career from papers and manuscripts left behind by Erickson. Beard helped me confirm the facts in this book.

Robert Workman, *Float Planes and Flying Boats*, (Annapolis: Naval Institute Press, 2012)

Coast Guard Aviation Association: Home Page - https://aoptero.org

Illustration/Photo Credits

The illustrations in this book are the original work of Matthew Melillo.

All the illustrations of historical images are based upon photos which depict the work of sailors or employees of the U.S. Coast Guard and U.S. Navy, taken or made as part of that person's official duties. As a work of the U.S. federal government, the images are in the public domain in the United States.

The aircraft photographs used in *Appendix B - Past and Present Coast Guard Aircraft* are also USCG photographs and in the public domain in the United States with the following exceptions:

•Page 41: Leoning Amphibian, left hand picture - Courtesy Peggy McCleskey, 1934

•Page 44: Sikorsky R-4, HNS-1, Hoverfly - Courtesy Robert Kastner from *WWII Pacific Eagles* by Jeff Ethell and Warren Bodie.

Sikorsky quote by AZ Quotes - Used with permission.

Meet the Author

James "Jim" Burd Brewster is a retired Coast Guard Officer who operated a Polar Icebreaker, helped plan and buy the USCGC Mackinaw, and organized the Coast Guard's participation in the 50th Anniversary of World War II. He is the author of the acclaimed "Glad to do it!" series of children's picture books featuring Uncle Rocky, Fireman and Officer Jack. His next project is to add EMT Morales to the series. He and Katie live outside of Washington, DC where they are visited by their five grown children and five grandchildren. Jim's heart still flutters whenever his three favorite ladies (Wife Katie, Daughter Rachel, Granddaughter Felicity) smile at him.

He can be contacted through: www.gladtodoit.net

Meet the Illustrator

Matthew Melillo (b.1989) is an American illustrator, born and raised in New Jersey, USA. He received his BFA from The School of Visual Arts (New York City) in 2011. Classically trained in all mediums, he works primarily digitally, combining elements of both photorealism and colorful abstraction.

He can be contacted through: www.melillodesign.com.